Italian Short Stories for Beginners Book 1

Over 100 Dialogues and Daily Used Phrases to Learn Italian in Your Car. Have Fun & Grow Your Vocabulary, with Crazy Effective Language Learning Lessons

www.LearnLikeNatives.com

www.LearnLikeNatives.com

© Copyright 2020
By Learn Like A Native

ALL RIGHTS RESERVED

No part of this book may be reproduced, stored in a retrieval system, or transmitted in any form or by any means, without the prior written permission of the publisher.

www.LearnLikeNatives.com

TABLE OF CONTENT

INTRODUCTION	5
CHAPTER 1 The Mysterious Package / Greetings	17
Translation of the Story	34
The Mysterious Package	34
CHAPTER 2 Mardi Gras / Colors + Days of the Week	43
Translation of the Story	57
Mardi Gras	57
CHAPTER 3 Weird Weather / Weather	65
Translation of the Story	79
Weird Weather	79
CONCLUSION	87
About the Author	93

www.LearnLikeNatives.com

www.LearnLikeNatives.com

INTRODUCTION

Before we dive into some Italian, I want to congratulate you, whether you're just beginning, continuing, or resuming your language learning journey. Here at Learn Like a Native, we understand the determination it takes to pick up a new language and after reading this book, you'll be another step closer to achieving your language goals.

As a thank you for learning with us, we are giving you free access to our 'Speak Like a Native' eBook. It's packed full of practical advice and insider tips on how to make language learning quick, easy, and most importantly, enjoyable. Head over to LearnLikeNatives.com to access your free guide and peruse our huge selection of language learning resources.

Learning a new language is a bit like cooking—you need several different ingredients and the right technique, but the end result is sure to be delicious. We created this book of short stories for learning Italian because language is alive. Language is about the senses—hearing, tasting the words on your tongue, and touching another culture up close. Learning a language in a classroom is a fine place to start, but it's not a complete introduction to a language.

In this book, you'll find a language come to life. These short stories are miniature immersions into the Italian language, at a level that is perfect for beginners. This book is not a lecture on grammar. It's not an endless vocabulary list. This book is the closest you can come to a language immersion without leaving the country. In the stories within, you will see people speaking to each other, going through daily life situations, and using the most common, helpful words and phrases in language.

www.LearnLikeNatives.com

You are holding the key to bringing your Italian studies to life.

Made for Beginners

We made this book with beginners in mind. You'll find that the language is simple, but not boring. Most of the book is in the present tense, so you will be able to focus on dialogues, root verbs, and understand and find patterns in subject-verb agreement.

This is not "just" a translated book. While reading novels and short stories translated into Italian is a wonderful thing, beginners (and even novices) often run into difficulty. Literary licenses and complex sentence structure can make reading in your second language truly difficult—not to mention BORING. That's why Italian Short

Stories for Beginners is the perfect book to pick up. The stories are simple, but not infantile. They were not written for children, but the language is simple so that beginners can pick it up.

The Benefits of Learning a Second Language

If you have picked up this book, it's likely that you are already aware of the many benefits of learning a second language. Besides just being fun, knowing more than one language opens up a whole new world to you. You will be able to communicate with a much larger chunk of the world. Opportunities in the workforce will open up, and maybe even your day-to-day work will be improved.

www.LearnLikeNatives.com

Improved communication can also help you expand your business. And from a neurological perspective, learning a second language is like taking your daily vitamins and eating well, for your brain!

How To Use The Book

The chapters of this book all follow the same structure:

- A short story with several dialogs
- A summary in Italian
- A list of important words and phrases and their English translation
- Questions to test your understanding
- Answers to check if you were right
- The English translation of the story to clear every doubt

www.LearnLikeNatives.com

You may use this book however is comfortable for you, but we have a few recommendations for getting the most out of the experience. Try these tips and if they work for you, you can use them on every chapter throughout the book.

1) Start by reading the story all the way through. Don't stop or get hung up on any particular words or phrases. See how much of the plot you can understand in this way. We think you'll get a lot more of it than you may expect, but it is completely normal not to understand everything in the story. You are learning a new language, and that takes time.

2) Read the summary in Italian. See if it matches what you have understood of the plot.

3) Read the story through again, slower this time. See if you can pick up the meaning of any words or phrases you don't understand

by using context clues and the information from the summary.

4) Test yourself! Try to answer the five comprehension questions that come at the end of each story. Write your answers down, and then check them against the answer key. How did you do? If you didn't get them all, no worries!

5) Look over the vocabulary list that accompanies the chapter. Are any of these the words you did not understand? Did you already know the meaning of some of them from your reading?

6) Now go through the story once more. Pay attention this time to the words and phrases you haven't understand. If you'd like, take the time to look them up to expand your meaning of the story. Every time you read over the story, you'll understand more and more.

7) Move on to the next chapter when you are ready.

Read and Listen

The audio version is the best way to experience this book, as you will hear a native Italian speaker tell you each story. You will become accustomed to their accent as you listen along, a huge plus for when you want to apply your new language skills in the real world.

If this has ignited your language learning passion and you are keen to find out what other resources are available, go to LearnLikeNatives.com, where you can access our vast range of free learning materials. Don't know where to begin? An excellent place to start is our 'Speak Like a Native' free eBook, full of practical advice and insider tips on how to make language learning quick, easy, and most importantly, enjoyable.

www.LearnLikeNatives.com

And remember, small steps add up to great advancements! No moment is better to begin learning than the present.

www.LearnLikeNatives.com

FREE BOOK!

Get the *FREE BOOK* that reveals the secrets path to learn any language fast, and without leaving your country.

Discover:

- The **language 5 golden rules** to master languages at will

- Proven **mind training techniques** to revolutionize your learning

- A complete step-by-step guide to **conquering any language**

www.LearnLikeNatives.com

www.LearnLikeNatives.com

CHAPTER 1
The Mysterious Package / Greetings

STORIA

Suona il campanello della porta.

Andrea corre alla porta dell'appartamento. Il campanello non suona mai il sabato mattina. Andrea è curioso di vedere chi è alla porta. Apre la porta.

"**Buongiorno**, ragazzino", dice un fattorino. L'uomo indossa un'uniforme marrone e ha con sé una scatola marrone.

"**Salve**, signore", dice Andrea.

"Ho un **pacco**," dice il fattorino. "Indirizzato a Via Roma, 10."

"Questa è Via Roma 10", dice Andrea.

"Sul pacco non c'è un nome," dice il fattorino. "Inoltre non ha il numero dell'appartamento."

"Che strano!" dice Andrea.

"Puoi darlo tu alla persona giusta?" chiede l'uomo.

"Posso provarci", dice Andrea. Ha solo dieci anni, ma si sente importante.

"**Grazie mille**", dice il fattorino. E se ne va. Andrea porta la scatola a casa sua. Fissa la scatola. Ha la dimensione di una scatola di scarpe. Non ha nome all'esterno, solo Via Roma, 10.

Andrea apre la scatola di cartone. Deve sapere cosa c'è dentro per trovare il proprietario. C'è una piccola scatola di legno all'interno della scatola di cartone. Andrea apre la scatola di legno. All'interno della scatola ci sono 10 paia di **occhiali** diversi. Sono di colori diversi: rosa e rosso, pois verdi, neri e bianchi. Hanno anche forme diverse: rotonde, quadrate e rettangolari.

Chiude la scatola e si mette le scarpe.

"**Ciao** mamma! Torno subito", grida.

Andrea bussa alla porta di fronte al corridoio dalla sua casa. La porta si apre. Una signora molto anziana sorride ad Andrea e alla scatola.

"**Buongiorno**, Signora Bianchi!" dice Andrea.

"**Come stai**?" chiede l'**anziana signora**.

"**Bene, grazie! E lei**?" dice Andrea.

"Che cos'hai in mano?" chiede la l'anziana signora.

"**Signora**, questo è un pacchetto. Appartiene a qualcuno in questo edificio, ma non so a chi", dice Andrea.

"Non è per me", dice la l'anziana signora. "Ne sono sicura!"

"Ah, ok" dice Andrea, deluso. L'anziana signora porta gli occhiali. Pensa che questi occhiali starebbero bene su di lei. Si gira per andarsene.

"Torna più tardi," dice l'anziana signora. "Sto facendo dei biscotti e alcuni sono per te e la tua famiglia."

Andrea sale le scale. Il suo edificio ha tre piani. È amico di quasi tutti nell'edificio. Tuttavia, l'appartamento al secondo piano c'è una nuova famiglia. Andrea non li conosce. Si sente timido, ma suona il campanello. Un uomo dai capelli castani apre la porta. Sorride.

"**Ciao**!" Esclama l'uomo.

"Ciao", risponde Andrea. "Vivo di sotto. **Mi chiamo** Andrea."

"**È un piacere conoscerti**, Andrea," dice l'uomo. "Siamo nuovi nell'edificio. Sono il Sigonor Jones."

"**Anche per me è un piacere conoscerti**", dice Andrea. "Questo pacchetto appartiene a qualcuno di questo edificio. È il tuo pacchetto?"

"Impossibile!" dice l'uomo. "Io e la mia famiglia ci siamo appena trasferiti qui. Nessuno conosce il nostro indirizzo."

"Ok," dice Andrea. "Piacere di averti conosciuto allora." La porta si chiude. Un altro no. Ci sono solo due appartamenti rimasti da provare. Nel prossimo appartamento c'è una famiglia. La figlia va alla stessa scuola di Andrea. Lei è un anno più grande di Andrea. Il suo nome è Diana. Andrea pensa che sia molto bella. Si sente di nuovo in **imbarazzo**, ma bussa alla porta.

Una bella bambina bionda apre la porta.

"**Ehilà**, Diana," sorride Andrea.

"**Come va**?" dice Diana. Il suo pigiama è rosa brillante e i suoi capelli sono disordinati.

"Bene grazie. E tu?" chiede Andrea.

"**Tutto bene**." dice Diana. "Stavo dormendo. Mi hai svegliato."

"Mi dispiace," dice velocemente. Il suo viso arrossisce. Si sente in soggezione. "Ho un pacchetto. Ma non so a chi appartiene."

"Cosa c'è dentro?" chiede Diana.

"Alcuni occhiali. Sono occhiali da lettura", dice Andrea.

"Non porto gli occhiali. Mia madre non li usa. La scatola non è per noi", dice Diana.

"Va bene", dice Andrea. Saluta e sale le scale. C'è un altro appartamento, l'appartamento al terzo piano. Il Signor Brambilla vive in questo appartamento, da solo. Ha un grande pappagallo che sa parlare. Ha anche quattro gatti e un cane. Il suo appartamento è vecchio e buio. Andrea ha paura del Signor Brambilla. Suona il campanello. Deve scoprire a chi appartiene la scatola.

"Ciao", dice il Signor Brambilla. Il suo cane arriva alla porta. Il cane aiuta il Signor Brambilla perché è cieco.

"Salve, Signor Brambilla. Sono Andrea," esclama Andrea. Il Signor Brambilla ha gli occhi chiusi. Sorride.

"Cosa c'è, Andrea?" Chiede. Hmmm, Andrea pensa, forse il Signor Brambilla non fa così paura. Forse il Signor Brambilla è solo un anziano signore che vive da solo.

"Ho un pacco e penso che sia per lei", dice Andrea.

"Ah sì! I miei occhiali da lettura. Finalmente!" sorride Il Signor Brambilla. E allunga le mani. Andrea è confuso e Guarda il cane. Sembra anche sorridere. Dà la scatola al Signor Brambilla.

"**Grazie, sei stato molto gentile**", dice il Signor Brambilla.

"**Si figuri**", dice Andrea. Forse visiterà il Signor Brambilla un altro giorno. Si gira e torna a casa.

RIASSUNTO

Un ragazzo, Andrea, ottiene un pacchetto non destinato a lui. Si tratta di una scatola di occhiali. La porta ai vicini, uno per uno, per scoprire a chi appartiene il pacco. Scopre che il pacco appartiene al suo vicino il Signor Brambilla, il che è un po' sorprendente.

LISTA DI VOCABOLI

Buongiorno	Good morning
Salve	Hello
Grazie mille	Thank you very much
Ciao	Hi
Occhiali	Glasses

Come stai?	How are you?
Bene, grazie! E tu?	Fine, thanks! And you?
Signora	Lady
Signore	Sir
Ehilà	Hello there
È un piacere conoscerti	Nice to meet you
Anche per me è un piacere conoscerti	It's nice to meet you too
Come va?	What's up?
Tutto bene	All is well

Imbarazzo	Embarrassment
Grazie, sei stato molto gentile	Thank you, you were very kind
Si figuri	My pleausere
Mi chiamo Andrea	My name is Andrea
Pacco	Package
Anziana signora	Old lady

DOMANDE

1. Chi c'è alla porta d'ingresso quando Andrea la apre?

    a) un fattorino

    b) un gatto

    c) una persona incaricata del censimento

    d) suo padre

2. Come descriveresti la Signora Bianchi?

    a) una bella ragazza

    b) una persona cattiva

    c) un vicino cattivo

    d) un'anziana signora e gentile

3. Chi vive al secondo piano del condominio?

    a) nessuno

    b) una ragazza della scuola di Andrea

    c) una nuova famiglia

    d) Andrea

4. Cosa pensa Andrea di Diana?

    a) gli piace e pensa che sia carina

    b) la segue sui social media

    c) non gli piace

    d) non si conoscono

5. A chi appartengono gli occhiali?

    a) alla vecchia signora

b) al Signore che ci vede poco

c) Ad Andrea e la sua famiglia

d) A nessuno

RISPOSTE

1. Chi c'è alla porta d'ingresso quando Andrea la apre?

   a) un fattorino

2. Come descriveresti la Signora Bianchi?

   d) un'anziana signora e gentile

3. Chi vive al secondo piano del condominio?

   c) una nuova famiglia

4. Cosa pensa Andrea di Diana?

   a) gli piace e pensa che sia carina

5. A chi appartengono gli occhiali?

   b) al Signore che ci vede poco

Translation of the Story

The Mysterious Package

The doorbell rings.

Andrew runs to the door of the apartment. The doorbell never rings on Saturday mornings. Andrew is excited to see who is at the door. He opens the door.

"**Good morning**, little boy," says a delivery man. The man is dressed in a brown uniform and is carrying a brown box.

"**Hello, sir**," says Andrew.

"I have a package," the delivery man says. "It says 10 Main Street."

"This is 10 Main Street," says Andrew.

"The package has no name," says the delivery man. "It also has no apartment number."

"How strange!" says Andrew.

"Can you give it to the right person?" the man asks.

"I can try," says Andrew. He is only ten years old, but he feels important.

"Thank you very much," says the delivery man. He leaves. Andrew takes the box into his house. He stares at the box. It is about the size of a shoe box. It has no name on the outside, just 10 Main Street.

Andrew opens the cardboard box. He needs to know what is inside to find the owner. There is a small wood box inside the cardboard box. Andrew opens the wooden box. Inside the box are 10 different pairs of eyeglasses. They are different colors: pink and red, green polka dots, black and white. They are also different shapes: round, square and rectangle.

He closes the box and puts on his shoes.

"**Bye** mom! I'll be right back," he shouts.

Andrew knocks on the door across the hall from his house. It opens. A very old lady smiles at Andrew and the box.

"**Morning**, Mrs. Smith!" says Andrew.

"**How are you?**" asks the old lady.

"**Fine, thanks! And you?**" says Andrew.

"What do you have?" asks the old lady.

"**Ma'am,** this is a package. It belongs to someone in this building but I don't know who," says Andrew.

"It's not for me," says the old lady. "Impossible!"

"Oh, ok" says Andrew, disappointed. The old lady wears glasses. He thinks these glasses would look nice on her. He turns to leave.

"Come back later," calls the old lady. "I'm making cookies and some cookies are for you and your family."

Andrew goes up the stairs. His building has three floors. He is friends with almost everyone in the building. However, the apartment on the second floor has a new family. Andrew doesn't know them. He feels shy, but he rings the bell. A brown-haired man opens the door. He smiles.

"**Hi!**" says the man.

"Hello," says Andrew. "I live downstairs. **My name is** Andrew."

"**It's nice to meet you,** Andrew," the man says. "We are new to the building. I'm Mr. Jones."

"**Nice to meet you too,**" says Andrew. "This package belongs to someone in this building. Is it your package?"

"Impossible!" says the man. "My family and I just moved here. No one knows our address."

"Ok," says Andrew. "Nice to meet you then." The door closes. Another no. There are only two apartments left to try. In the next apartment is a family. The daughter goes to the same school as Andrew. She is a year older than Andrew. Her name is Diana. Andrew thinks she is very beautiful. He feels shy again, but he knocks on the door.

A pretty, blonde girl opens the door.

"**Hey,** Diana," Andrew smiles.

"What's up?" Diana says. Her pijamas are bright pink and her hair is messy.

"How's it going?" Andrew asks.

"It's going," Diana says. "I was asleep. You woke me up."

"I'm sorry," he says quickly. His face is red. He feels extra shy. "I have a package. We don't know who it belongs to."

"What is in it?" asks Diana.

"Some glasses. They are glasses for reading," says Andrew.

"I don't wear glasses. My mom doesn't use them. The box is not for us," says Diana.

"Ok," says Andrew. He waves goodbye and climbs the stairs. There is one more apartment, the apartment on the third floor. Mr. Edwards lives in this apartment, alone. He has a big parrot that knows how to talk. He also has four cats and a dog. His apartment is old and dark. Andrew feels afraid of Mr. Edwards. He rings the doorbell. He has to find out who the box belongs to.

"Hello," says Mr. Edwards. His dog comes to the door. The dog helps Mr. Edwards because he is blind.

"Hi, Mr. Edwards. It's Andrew," Andrew says. Mr. Edwards has his eyes closed. He smiles.

"What's new, Andrew?" He asks. Hmmm, Andrew thinks, maybe Mr. Edwards isn't scary. Maybe Mr. Edwards is just a nice old man that lives alone.

"I have a package and I think it is for you," says Andrew.

"Ah yes! My reading glasses. Finally!" smiles Mr. Edwards. He holds his hands out. Andrew is confused. He looks at the dog. It seems to be smiling, too. He gives Mr. Edwards the box.

"It's good to see you," says Mr. Edwards.

"You too," says Andrew. Maybe he will visit Mr. Edwards another day. He turns around and goes home.

CHAPTER 2
Mardi Gras / Colors + Days of the Week

Franco esce dalla sua porta di casa. La sua nuova casa è **viola** con le finestre **blu**. I **colori** sono molto luminosi per essere una casa. A New Orleans, la sua nuova città, gli edifici sono colorati.

Egli è nuovo nel quartiere. Franco non ha ancora amici. La casa accanto alla sua è un alto edificio **rosso**. Una famiglia vive lì. Franco fissa la porta e un uomo la apre. Franco lo saluta.

"Ciao, vicino di casa!" dice Giorgio. Saluta. Franco cammina verso la casa rossa.

"Ciao, sono Franco, il nuovo vicino", dice Franco.

"Piacere di conoscerti. Il mio nome è Giorgio," dice Giorgio. Gli uomini si stringono la mano. Giorgio ha una serie di luci nelle sue mani. Le luci sono **verdi**, **viola** e **oro**.

"A cosa servono le luci?" chiede Franco.

"Sei nuovo," ride Giorgio. "È Martedì Grasso, non lo sapevi? Questi colori rappresentano la festa del carnevale qui a New Orleans."

"Oh, sì", dice Franco. Franco non sa nulla del carnevale. Non ha nemmeno amici con cui fare progetti.

"Oggi è **venerdì**", dice Giorgio. "C'è una parata chiamata Endymion. Vieni con me e la famiglia a guardare?"

"Sì", dice Franco. "Fantastico!"

Giorgio mette le luci sulla casa e Franco aiuta Giorgio. Giorgio accende le luci. La casa sembra festosa.

La famiglia e Franco vanno alla parata. Durante il Martedì Grasso a New Orleans, ci sono sfilate ogni giorno. Le sfilate durante la **settimana** sono piccole. Le sfilate del fine settimana, **sabato** e

domenica, sono grandi, con molti carri e persone. C'è un re del Martedì Grasso. Il suo nome è Rex.

Mardi Gras significa **Martedì** Grasso. In Inghilterra, si chiama Shrove Tuesday. È una festa cattolica. È il giorno prima del **Mercoledì** delle Ceneri, l'inizio della Quaresima. Martedì Grasso è la celebrazione prima della Quaresima, un momento serio. Da **giovedì**, i giorni speciali sono finiti. New Orleans è famosa per il suo Martedì Grasso. La gente fa feste e indossa maschere e costumi. Infatti, a New Orleans si può indossare una maschera solo il Martedì Grasso. Il resto dell'anno è illegale!

Giorgio e la sua famiglia guardano la parata iniziare insieme a Franco. Franco è sorpreso. Ci sono molte persone che guardano. Stanno lì, in piedi nell'erba. I carri di carnevale passano davanti al gruppo. I carri di carnevale sono grandi strutture con persone e decorazioni. Sfilano per la strada, uno per uno.

Il primo carro di carnevale rappresenta il sole. Ha decorazioni **gialle**. Una donna nel mezzo indossa un abito **bianco**. Sembra un angelo. Lancia coriandoli **arancioni** e perline alla gente.

"Perché lancia coriandoli e collane?" chiede Franco.

"Per noi!" dice Hannah, la moglie di Giorgio. Hannah tiene cinque collane tra le mani. Alcune perline sono per terra. Nessuno le prende. Sono sporche e di colore **marrone**.

La parata continua. Ci sono molti carri di carnevale, e molte perline. Giorgio e la sua famiglia gridano: "Buttami qualcosa!" Anna riempie la sua borsa **nera** di giocattoli colorati e perline dai carri. Franco impara a gridare "Gettami qualcosa!" per prendere anche lui delle perline.

Un grande carro ha più di 250 persone su di esso. E 'il più grande del mondo.

Infine, la parata finisce. I bambini e gli adulti sono felici. Tutti vanno a casa. Franco è molto stanco. Ha anche fame e vuole mangiare. Segue Giorgio e la sua famiglia nella casa rossa. C'è una grande torta rotonda sul tavolo. Sembra un anello, con un buco al centro. La torta ha una glassa viola, verde e gialla che la ricopre.

"Questa è la torta del re", dice Hannah. "Mangiamo la torta del re ogni Martedì Grasso."

Hannah taglia un pezzo di torta. Dà un pezzo a Giorgio, un pezzo ai bambini, e un pezzo a Franco. Franco assaggia la torta. È delizioso! Sa di cannella ed è morbida. Ma Franco morde improvvisamente nella plastica.

"Ahia!" dice Franco. Franco smette di mangiare. Tira fuori un bambino di plastica dalla torta.

"C'è un'altra tradizione," dice Giorgio. "La torta ha un bambino in esso. La persona che ottiene il bambino compra la prossima torta."

"Sono io!" dice Franco.

Tutti ridono. Giorgio invita Franco a un'altra parata **lunedì**.

Franco torna a casa felice. Ama già il Martedì Grasso.

RIASSUNTO

Franco è nuovo nel quartiere. Incontra i suoi vicini e festeggiano il Carnevale insieme a New Orleans. Franco è stupito dai carri allegorici e dalle parate. Tornano a casa per mangiare la torta del re e Franco ha una sorpresa.

www.LearnLikeNatives.com

LISTA DI VOCABOLI

Lilla	violet
Blu	blue
Colori	colors
Rosso	red
Verde	green
Viola	purple
Oro	gold
Venerdì	Friday
Settimana	week

Sabato	Saturday
Domenica	Sunday
Martedì	Tuesday
Mercoledi	Wednesday
Giovedi	Thursday
Giallo	yellow
Bianco	white
Arancione	orange
Marrone	brown
Nero	black
Lunedì	Monday

www.LearnLikeNatives.com

DOMANDE

1) Come descriveresti la nuova casa di Franco?

    a) noiosa

    b) colorata

    c) minuscola

    d) solitaria

2) Quale colore rappresenta il Martedì Grasso a New Orleans?

    a) blu

    b) bianco

    c) arancione

    d) oro

3) Martedì Grasso è una festa:

    a) solo per adulti.

    b) dalla tradizione della chiesa ebraica.

    c) molto famosa a New Orleans.

    d) che si fa in casa.

4) Quali di questi non sono sul carro del Martedì Grasso?

    a) persone

    b) computer

    c) coriandoli

    d) perline

5) Cosa succede se si trova il bambino in una torta del re?

a) tu piangi

b) è necessario prendersi cura del bambino

c) devi darlo a un tuo amico

d) la prossima volta devi acquistare una torta del re

RISPOSTE

1) Come descriverebbe la nuova casa di Franco?

a) colorata

2) Quale colore rappresenta il Martedì Grasso a New Orleans?

d) oro

3) Martedì Grasso è una festa:

c) molto famosa a New Orleans.

4) Quali di questi non sono sul carro del Martedì Grasso?

b) computer

5) Cosa succede se si trova il bambino in una torta re?

d) la prossima volta devi acquistare una torta del re

www.LearnLikeNatives.com

Translation of the Story

Mardi Gras

STORY

Frank steps out his front door. His new house is **violet** with **blue** windows. The **colors** are very bright for a house. In New Orleans, his new home, buildings are colorful.

He is new to the neighborhood. Frank does not have any friends yet. The house next to him is a tall, **red** building. A family lives there. Frank stares at the door, and a man opens it. Frank says hello.

"Hello, neighbor!" says George. He waves. Frank walks to the red house.

"Hi, I'm Frank, the new neighbor," says Frank.

"Nice to meet you. My name is George," George says. The men shake hands. George has a string of lights in his hands. The lights are **green**, **purple** and **gold**.

"What are the lights for?" asks Frank.

"You *are* new," laughs George. "It's Mardi Gras, didn't you know? These colors represent the holiday of carnival here in New Orleans."

"Oh, yes," says Frank. Frank does not know about carnival. He also has no friends to make plans with.

"Today is **Friday**," says George. "There is a parade called Endymion. Will you come with me and the family to watch?"

"Yes," Frank says. "Wonderful!"

George puts the lights on the house. Frank helps George. George turns on the lights. The house looks festive.

The family and Frank go to the parade. During Mardi Gras in New Orleans, there are parades every day. The parades during the **week** are small. The parades on the weekend, **Saturday** and **Sunday**, are big, with many floats and people. There is a king of Mardi Gras. His name is Rex.

Mardi Gras means 'Fat **Tuesday'.** In England, it is called Shrove Tuesday. The holiday is Catholic. It is one day before Ash **Wednesday**, the beginning of Lent. Mardi Gras is the celebration before Lent, a serious time. By **Thursday**, the special days are finished. New Orleans is famous for its Mardi Gras. People have parties and wear masks and costumes. In fact, you can only wear a mask in New Orleans on Mardi Gras. The rest of the year it is illegal!

George and his family watch the parade begin with Frank. Frank is surprised. There are many people watching. They stand in the grass. Floats pass the group. Floats are big structures with people and decorations. They go down the street, one by one.

The first float represents the sun. It has **yellow** decorations. A woman in the middle wears a **white** dress. She looks like an angel. She throws **orange** toys and beads to the people.

"Why does she throw the toys and necklaces?" asks Frank.

"For us!" says Hannah, George's wife. Hannah holds five necklaces in her hands. Some beads are on the ground. Nobody catches them. They are dirty and **brown**.

The parade continues. There are many floats, and many beads. George and his family shout, "Throw me something, mister!" Hannah fills her **black** bag with colorful toys and beads from the floats. Frank learns to shout "Throw me something!" to get beads for himself.

One big float has over 250 people on it. It is the largest in the world.

Finally, the parade ends. The children and the adults are happy. Everyone goes home. Frank is tired. He is also hungry and wants to eat. He follows George and his family into the **red** house. There is a big, round cake on the table. It looks like a ring, with a hole in the middle. The cake has **purple**, **green** and **yellow** frosting on top.

"This is king cake," Hannah says. "We eat king cake every Mardi Gras."

Hannah cuts a piece of cake. She gives one piece to George, one piece to the children, and one piece to Frank. Frank tastes the cake. It is delicious! It tastes like cinnamon. It is soft. But suddenly Frank bites into plastic.

"Ouch!" says Frank. Frank stops eating. He pulls a plastic baby out of the cake.

"There is one more tradition," says George. "The cake has a baby in it. The person who gets the baby buys the next cake."

"That's me!" Frank says.

Everyone laughs. George invites Frank to another parade on **Monday.**

Frank goes home happy. He loves Mardi Gras.

www.LearnLikeNatives.com

CHAPTER 3
Weird Weather / Weather

Ivan ha dodici anni. Visita i nonni nel fine settimana. Ama visitare i nonni. La nonna gli dà biscotti e latte ogni giorno. Il nonno gli insegna cose carine. Questo fine settimana va a casa loro.

È febbraio, ed è **inverno**. A febbraio, di solito nevica e Ivan ama la **neve**. Ci gioca e si diverte con le palle di neve. Questo fine settimana di febbraio, il **tempo** è diverso. Il sole splende; è **soleggiato** e quasi **caldo**! Ivan è a casa dei nonni e indossa una maglietta.

"Ciao, nonno! Ciao, nonna!" esclama Ivan.

"Ciao, Ivan!" dice la nonna.

"Ivan! Come stai?" dice il nonno.

"Sto bene", dice, e abbraccia i nonni. Ivan saluta sua madre che lo ha accompagnato.

Entrano in casa. "Questo tempo è strano," dice la nonna. "Febbraio è sempre freddo e **nuvoloso**. Non capisco!"

"È il **cambiamento climatico**", dice Ivan. A scuola Ivan impara la contaminazione e l'inquinamento. Il tempo cambia a causa di cambiamenti nell'atmosfera. Il cambiamento climatico è il mutare del clima nel tempo.

"Non conosco il cambiamento climatico," dice il nonno. "**Prevedo** il tempo da quello che vedo."

"Cosa vuoi dire?" chiede Ivan.

"Questa mattina, il **cielo** è rosso," dice il nonno. "Questo significa che so che sta arrivando una **tempesta**."

"Come?" chiede Ivan.

"Cielo rosso di mattina, la pioggia si avvicina. Cielo rosso di sera, bel tempo si spera," Dice il Nonno a Ivan.

Se il cielo è rosso all'alba, significa che c'è acqua nell'aria. La luce del sole brilla di rosso. La tempesta viene verso di voi. Se il cielo è rosso al tramonto, il maltempo si sta allontanando. Senza **meteorologi**, la gente guarda il cielo per avere indizi sul tempo.

"Come fanno i meteorologi a prevedere il tempo?" chiede Ivan.

"osservano le caratteristiche dell'atmosfera", dice la nonna. "Osservano la temperatura, se è calda o fredda. E osservano la pressione dell'aria, ciò che sta accadendo nell'atmosfera."

"Io Prevedo il meteo in modo diverso", dice il nonno. "Ad esempio, so che oggi pioverà."

"Come?" chiede Ivan.

"Il gatto", dice il nonno. Ivan guarda il gatto. Il gatto apre la bocca e dice 'ah-CHUU'.

"Quando il gatto starnutisce o russa, significa che la pioggia sta arrivando," dice il nonno. Può **piovigginare** o può essere molto **piovoso**, ma pioverà."

Improvvisamente, sentono un suono forte. Ivan guarda fuori dalla finestra. Le gocce di pioggia stanno cadendo forte. La pioggia è forte. Ivan non riesce a sentire quello che dice il nonno.

"Cosa?" dice Ivan.

"**Sta piovendo a dirotto**", dice il nonno, sorridendo.

"Ah!" ride Ivan.

"Conosco un altro modo per capire il tempo", dice la nonna.

La nonna guarda i ragni per vedere quando farà freddo. Alla fine **dell'estate**, il tempo cambia. **L'autunno** porta aria fresca. La nonna sa che quando i ragni entrano all'interno, significa che il freddo sta arrivando. I ragni fanno una casa all'interno prima dell'inverno. È così che la nonna sa quando arriva il tempo invernale.

La pioggia si ferma. Nonno e Ivan escono. Nonno e nonna vivono in una casa nella foresta. La casa è circondata da alberi. Si tratta di una piccola casa. Ivan ha solo la sua maglietta e ha freddo. Il tempo non è soleggiato. L'aria si muove. È **ventosa** e soffia tra i capelli di Ivan.

"Fa **freddo** adesso", dice Ivan.

"Sì", dice il nonno. "Qual è la temperatura?"

"Non lo so," dice Ivan. "Non ho un termometro."

"Non ne hai bisogno", dice il nonno. Il nonno dice a Ivan di ascoltare. Ivan sente un suono: cri-cri-cri-cri. È un insetto. Il cri-cri-cri è il suono dei grilli. Insegna il nonno ad Ivan. Ivan conta il cri per otto secondi. Il Nonno aggiunge 5 a quel numero. Questa è la temperatura esterna. Ivan non sapeva che i grilli fossero come i termometri.

La nonna esce di casa. Sorride. Guarda Ivan contare il suono cri-cri. "Tempo per biscotti e latte!" dice.

"Evviva!" dice Ivan.

"Oh, guarda!" dice la nonna. "È un arcobaleno." L'arcobaleno va dalla casa alla foresta. Ha molti colori: rosso, arancione, giallo, blu e verde. L'arcobaleno è bellissimo. La Nonna, il Nonno e Ivan guardano l'arcobaleno. L'arcobaleno scompare e vanno dentro.

"Biscotti e latte per tutti", dice la nonna. Dà a Ivan un biscotto caldo al cioccolato.

"Non per me", dice il nonno. "Voglio il tè."

"Perché il tè?" dice la nonna. Ha due tazze di latte in mano.

"È inverno, dopo tutto", dice il nonno. Ride. Ivan e la nonna ridono con lui.

RIASSUNTO

Ivan passa il fine settimana con i nonni. È una giornata calda a febbraio. Parlano del tempo. I nonni di Ivan gli insegnano nuovi modi per prevedere il tempo. Ivan impara gli indizi che gli dà la natura. La famiglia va fuori per cercare di prevedere il tempo.

LISTA DI VOCABOLI

Inverno	winter
Nevicare	to snow
Clima	weather
Soleggiato	sunny
Caldo	hot
Freddo	cold
Nuvoloso	cloudy
Cambiamento climático	climate change
Atmosfera	atmosphere
Prevedere	predict

Cielo	sky
Temporale	storm
Mtereologo	weathermen
Pioviggina	drizzle
Piovoso	rainy
Pioggia a catinelle	raining cats and dogs
Estate	summer
Autunno	autumn
Ventoso	windy
Temperatura	temperature
Termómetro	thermometer

Arcobaleno	rainbow
Mal tempo	under the weather

DOMANDE

1) Com'è il tempo questo febbraio da Ivan?

    a) caldo

    b) freddo

    c) soleggiato

    d) fresco

2) Come fa il nonno a sapere come sarà il tempo?

    a) guarda la televisione

b) ascolta i meteorologi

c) osserva la natura

d) non predice il tempo

3) Che cosa significa quando i ragni entrano dentro?

a) hanno molta fame

b) sono pronti per deporre le uova

c) il freddo sta arrivando

d) il caldo sta arrivando

4) Perché il nonno chiede il tè invece del latte?

a) gli piace bere bevande calde in inverno

b) è allergico al latte

c) è estate

d) per far arrabbiare la nonna

RISPOSTE

1) Com'è il tempo a febbraio?

    a) caldo

2) Come fa il nonno a sapere come sarà il tempo?

    c) osserva la natura

3) Che cosa significa quando i ragni entrano dentro?

    c) il freddo sta arrivando

4) Perché il nonno chiede il tè invece del latte?

    a) gli piace bere bevande calde in inverno

www.LearnLikeNatives.com

Translation of the Story

Weird Weather

STORY

Ivan is twelve years old. He visits his grandparents on the weekend. He loves to visit his grandparents. Grandma gives him cookies and milk every day. Grandpa teaches him neat things. This weekend he goes to their house.

It is February. Where Ivan is, it is **winter**. In February, it usually **snows**. Ivan loves the snow. He plays in it and rolls it into balls. This February weekend, the **weather** is different. The sun is shining; it is **sunny** and almost **hot**! Ivan wears a T-shirt to his grandparent's house.

"Hi, Grandpa! Hi, Grandma!" Ivan says.

"Hello, Ivan!" Grandma says.

"Ivan! How are you?" says Grandpa.

"I'm good," he says, and he hugs his grandparents. Ivan says goodbye to his mom.

They go into the house. "This weather is strange," says Grandma. "February is always **cold** and **cloudy**. I don't understand!"

"It is **climate change**," says Ivan. In school, Ivan learns about contamination and pollution. The weather changes because of changes in the **atmosphere**. Climate change is the difference in the weather over time.

"I don't know about climate change," says Grandpa. "I **predict** the weather by what I see."

"What do you mean?" asks Ivan.

"This morning, the **sky** is red," says Grandpa. "This means I know a **storm** is coming."

"How?" asks Ivan.

"Red sky in the morning, sailors take warning. Red sky at night, sailor's delight." Grandpa tells Ivan about this saying.

If the sky is red at sunrise, it means there is water in the air. The light of the sun shines red. The storm is coming towards you. If the sky is red at sunset, the bad weather is leaving. Without **weathermen**, people watch the sky for clues about the weather.

"How do weathermen predict the weather?" asks Ivan.

"They look at patterns in the atmosphere," says Grandma. "They look at temperature, if it is hot or cold. And they look at air pressure, what is happening in the atmosphere."

"I predict the weather differently," says Grandpa. "For example, I know today it will **rain**."

"How?" asks Ivan.

"The cat," says Grandpa. Ivan looks at the cat. The cat opens its mouth and says 'ah-CHOO'.

"When the cat sneezes or snores, that means rain is coming," says Grandpa. It may **drizzle** or it may be very **rainy**, but it will rain."

Suddenly, they hear a loud sound. Ivan looks out the window. Drops of rain are falling hard. The rain is loud. Ivan can't hear what his Grandpa says.

"What?" says Ivan.

"It's **raining cats and dogs**," says Grandpa, smiling.

"Ha!" laughs Ivan.

"I know another way to tell the weather," says Grandma.

Grandma watches the spiders to see when the weather will be cold. At the end of **summer**, the weather changes. **Autumn** brings fresh, cool air. Grandma knows that when spiders come inside, it means cold weather is coming. The spiders make a house inside before winter. That is how grandma knows when the winter weather comes.

The rain stops. Grandpa and Ivan go out. Grandpa and Grandma live in a house in the forest. The house has trees around it. It is a small house. Ivan is cold in his T-shirt. The weather is not sunny. The air is moving. It is **windy**. The wind blows through Ivan's hair.

"It is **cold** now," says Ivan.

"Yes," says Grandpa. "What is the temperature?"

"I don't know," says Ivan. "I don't have a thermometer."

"You don't need one," says Grandpa. Grandpa tells Ivan to listen. Ivan hears a sound: *cri-cri-cri*. It is an insect. The *cri-cri-cri* is the sound of crickets. Grandpa teaches Ivan. Ivan counts the *cri* for fourteen seconds. Grandpa adds 40 to that number. That is the temperature outside. Ivan did not know crickets were like thermometers.

Grandma comes out of the house. She smiles. She watches Ivan counting the *cri* sound. "Time for cookies and milk!" she says.

"Yay!" says Ivan.

"Oh, look!" says Grandma. "It's a rainbow." The rainbow goes from the house to the forest. It has many colors: red, orange, yellow, blue and green. The rainbow is beautiful. Grandma, Grandpa and Ivan watch the rainbow. It disappears and they go inside.

"Cookies and milk for everyone," says Grandma. She gives Ivan a warm chocolate cookie.

"Not for me," says Grandpa. "I want tea."

"Why tea?" says Grandma. She has two milks in her hand.

"I'm feeling **under the weather**," says Grandpa. He laughs. Ivan and Grandma laugh with him.

CONCLUSION

You did it!

You finished a whole book in a brand new language. That in and of itself is quite the accomplishment, isn't it?

Congratulate yourself on time well spent and a job well done. Now that you've finished the book, you have familiarized yourself with over 500 new vocabulary words, comprehended the heart of 3 short stories, and listened to loads of dialogue unfold, all without going anywhere!

Charlemagne said "To have another language is to possess a second soul." After immersing yourself in this book, you are broadening your horizons and opening a whole new path for yourself.

Have you thought about how much you know now that you did not know before? You've learned everything from how to greet and how to express your emotions to basics like colors and place words. You can tell time and ask question. All without opening a schoolbook. Instead, you've cruised through fun, interesting stories and possibly listened to them as well.

Perhaps before you weren't able to distinguish meaning when you listened to Italian. If you used the audiobook, we bet you can now pick out meanings and words when you hear someone speaking. Regardless, we are sure you have taken an important step to being more fluent. You are well on your way!

Best of all, you have made the essential step of distinguishing in your mind the idea that most often hinders people studying a new language. By approaching Italian through our short stories and dialogs, instead of formal lessons with just grammar and vocabulary, you are no longer in the 'learning' mindset. Your approach is much more similar to an osmosis, focused on speaking and using the language, which is the end goal, after all!

So, what's next?

This is just the first of five books, all packed full of short stories and dialogs, covering essential, everyday Italian that will ensure you master the basics. You can find the rest of the books in the series, as well as a whole host of other resources, at LearnLikeNatives.com. Simply add the book to your library to take the next step in your language learning journey. If you are ever in need of new ideas or direction, refer to our 'Speak Like a Native' eBook, available to you for free at LearnLikeNatives.com, which clearly outlines practical steps you can take to continue learning any language you choose.

We also encourage you to get out into the real world and practice your Italian. You have a leg up on most beginners, after all—instead of pure textbook learning, you have been absorbing the sound and soul of the language. Do not underestimate the foundation you have built reviewing the chapters of this book. Remember, no one feels 100% confident when they speak with a native speaker in another language.

One of the coolest things about being human is connecting with others. Communicating with someone in their own language is a wonderful gift. Knowing the language turns you into a local and opens up your world. You will see the reward of learning languages for many years to come, so keep that practice up!. Don't let your fears stop you from taking the chance to use your Italian.

Just give it a try, and remember that you will make mistakes. However, these mistakes will teach you so much, so view every single one as a small victory! Learning is growth.

Don't let the quest for learning end here! There is so much you can do to continue the learning process in an organic way, like you did with this book. Add another book from Learn Like a Native to your library. Listen to Italian talk radio. Watch some of the great Italian films. Put on the latest CD from Pavarotti. Take cooking lessons in Italian. Whatever you do, don't stop because every little step you take counts towards learning a new language, culture, and way of communicating.

www.LearnLikeNatives.com

www.LearnLikeNatives.com

Learn Like a Native is a revolutionary **language education brand** that is taking the linguistic world by storm. Forget boring grammar books that never get you anywhere, Learn Like a Native teaches you languages in a fast and fun way that actually works!

As an international, multichannel, language learning platform, we provide **books, audio guides and eBooks** so that you can acquire the knowledge you need, swiftly and easily.

Our **subject-based learning**, structured around real-world scenarios, builds your conversational muscle and ensures you learn the content most relevant to your requirements. Discover our tools at *LearnLikeNatives.com*.

When it comes to learning languages, we've got you covered!

www.ingramcontent.com/pod-product-compliance
Lightning Source LLC
Chambersburg PA
CBHW071750080526
44588CB00013B/2206